I Wish My Students Knew

Jennifer Jones

I Wish My Students Knew

Jennifer Jones

I wish my students knew,
I'm excited for the school year to start.
I read the class names,
And feel warmth inside my heart.

I wish my students knew,
The butterflies I feel
The night before school begins,
I, too, am nervous for the ordeal.

I can barely sleep, I have the jitters,
I can't wait for the first day to start.
I look forward to the days we spend together,
And I miss them when we're apart.

I wish my students knew
How grateful I am for their participation.
Every time they raise their hands,
I feel so much appreciation.

I wish my students knew
How much their kind gestures make my day.
Sometimes it's how they are kind to each other,
Other times it's the kind things they say.

I wish my students knew
How much I love to see that they have learned.
Gaining knowledge in particular subjects
Is a benefit that they have earned.

I wish my students knew
That I am always rooting them on,
Especially in the subjects
Where they may feel not as strong.

Helping them solve challenging problems,
And coming to the answers on their own
Is the greatest feeling, as a teacher,
That I have ever known.

I wish my students knew
I see the effort in their tests.
Even if they don't get the answers right,
I know they are trying their best.

I wish my students knew
That I will never let them fail.
I am here to help them understand,
And work through all the little details.

I wish my students knew,
How much I love teaching throughout the year.
From fall until almost summer,
I'll be here for them, never fear.

I wish my students knew
That they can count on me.
When life gets them down,
I'll be a friend that they need.

I wish my students knew,
How deeply I care.
Whatever is going on in their lives,
I'll always be there.

I wish my students knew
I love them as if they are my family.
I know times may get tough,
But they are each so special to me.

I wish my students knew
How much they're on my mind.
How often I think about them
When their desks are left behind.

I wish my students knew,
Even when the day is done,
I work on all our lesson plans
To hopefully make learning fun.

I wish my students knew
How proud I am of each one,
I show them with a celebration
When the school year is done.

Even though they move up,
Through all the grades over time,
And while they may not be in my class anymore,
They will always be students of mine!

I love to hear from my readers. Write to me at
jenniferjonesbooks@gmail.com

Please visit chairsonstrike.com for the latest news
and updates on future titles!

www.ingramcontent.com/pod-product-compliance
Lightning Source LLC
Chambersburg PA
CBHW042025090426
42811CB00016B/1748

* 9 7 8 1 6 3 7 3 1 6 1 6 0 *